The Pest

by Tony Bradman
Illustrated by Bill Ledger

OXFORD

UNIVERSITY PRESS

In this story ...

Cam

Cam can turn into different animals.

Jin

Jin can zoom up and up.
He can go as high as a ro

Cam and Jin were out on the grass having a picnic.

"Have you seen my snack bar?" Jin said.
"I left it on the rug."

"Look! That squirrel has the snack bar,"
said Cam.

"No squirrel is going to run off with my snack bar!" Jin said.

Jin shot up in the air.

"I cannot fit in the gap," Jin said.
"It's too small!"

He landed with a soft bump.

"The squirrel has left bits of the snack bar," Cam said.

"This is a task for me!" Cam said. "I will turn into a robin."

Cam went to hunt for the lost snack bar.

Cam went to tell Jin.
"It is not a pest!" Cam said. "It has a
nest. We need to help it."

"This is a gift, just for you," Cam said to the squirrel.

"No need to pinch my snack bars from now on!" Jin said.

"You can have my snack bar, Jin!"
Cam said, with a grin.